TEACH YOURSELF TO PLAY

PIANO
SONGS

ALL ABOUT THAT BASS

In this Meghan Trainor mega-hit, it really **is** all about the bass! Begin with the left hand. There are three short bass riffs to learn, each with the same rhythm. The first one starts on A, the second, one note higher, on B. The third is a bit of a leap down to low E.

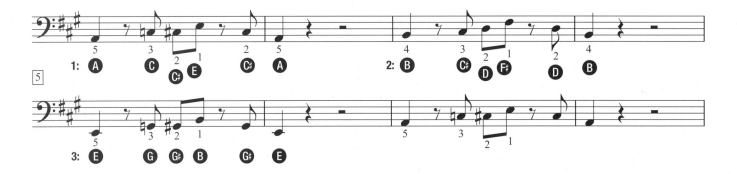

Something nifty comes up next. Those left-hand riffs continue, but now, each is repeated, so there are two measures starting on A, two starting on B, and two starting on low E. For the rest of the song, the left hand vamps on these short bass patterns. All you need to do is recognize which note to start on. Memorizing these, and using your ear, makes learning the left-hand part super easy.

Let's take a look at the melody. You'll see a lot of 6ths, for a little thinner texture than full chords to start with. Then, in measure 8 the right hand is notated with "x" note-heads, which denote a spoken rhythm. The melody picks up again with full chords at the end of measure 14. Although the two-measure phrases stay generally within an octave span, you'll need to move from place to place, as we've indicated on the example below. Notice how each hand aligns rhythmically with the other.

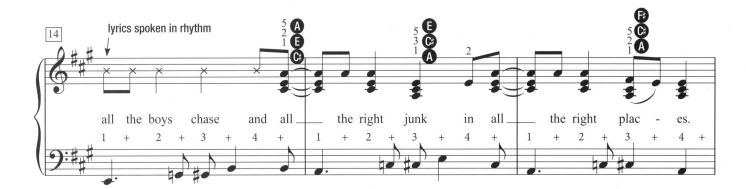

The next section, beginning at measure 25, is made of four-measure sequences. The top notes of the chords move in a downward scale pattern: A-G#-F#-E-D-C#.

Measures 29-32 move in the same way, this time starting on G#. The next eight measures are exactly the same as the previous eight, ending at the D.S. al Coda.

The coda winds down in thirds, with the left-hand riff continuing straight to the end. The thirds move down one note at a time, and we've added some fingering that will help you play this smoothly.

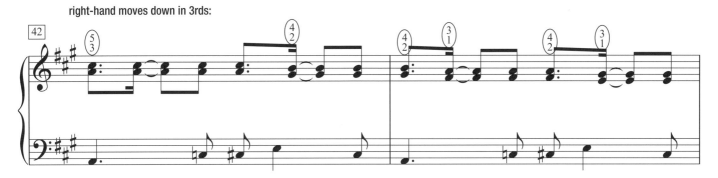

While the full chords in this arrangement might seem like a handful, there's lots of repetition, and the chords are close together on the keyboard. Always looks for similar notes between chords to keep your bearings.

Remember, the online audio has some neat features for learning this song. Play along with either hand, check your rhythms, and loop any sections that need extra work.

ALL ABOUT THAT BASS

Words and Music by KEVIN KADISH
and MEGHAN TRAINOR

Moderate groove

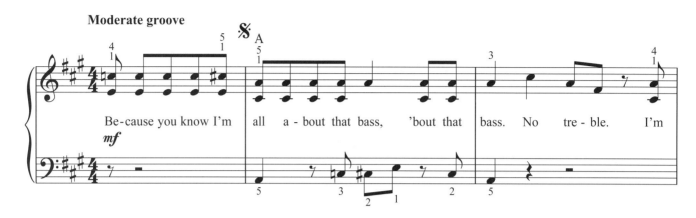

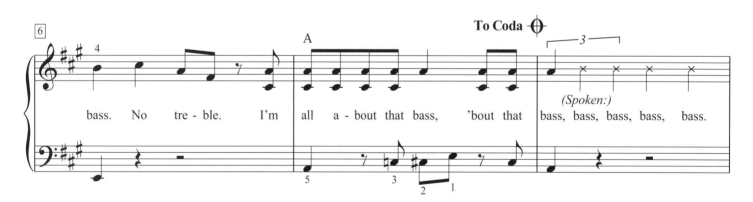

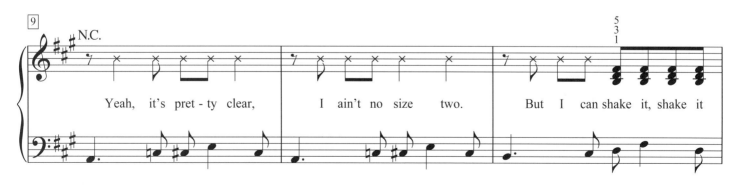

like I'm sup-posed to do. 'Cause I got that boom, boom that all the boys chase and all

the right junk in all the right plac - es. I see the mag - a - zine

work - in' that Pho - to - shop. We know that sh** ain't real.

C'-mon now, make it stop. If you got beau - ty, beau - ty, just raise 'em up 'cause ev - 'ry

ALL OF ME

This tender piano ballad opens simply, with right-hand 5ths and 6ths against single bass notes, setting the tone for the beautiful and sentimental lyrics. You'll play comfortably in the middle range of the keyboard, which also makes this easy to sing. The verse is rooted strongly in the chord progression E5-Cmaj7-G-D. You'll repeat these four chords three more times, taking you through measure 20. Take a closer look below, focusing on measures 5-8.

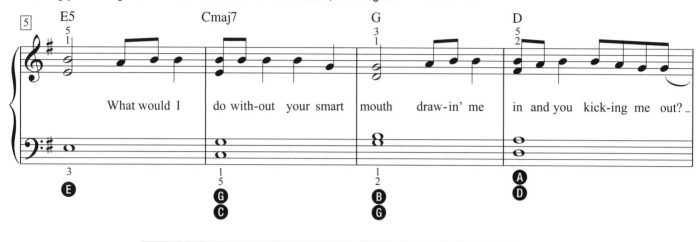

The rhythm eighth-quarter-eighth figures prominently in this tune, and fits the lyrics perfectly. Listen, and sing along with the audio if you need to review.

Measures 20-24 stay with a simple right-hand melody, but the left-hand chord progression varies slightly with the addition of the Am9 chord. The left hand plays the fifths **arpeggiated** or broken, instead of in the solid, blocked 5ths of the earlier measures.

The arpeggios continue between the hands in the chorus, beginning at measure 29. Notice how the right hand and left hand trade off, for a gentle, flowing feel. Check out the counting written in below to see just how the hands line up.

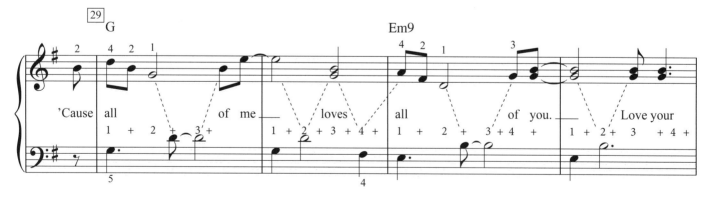

Measures 37-44 are a repeat of measures 29-36, so you're ready to look ahead to the ending. Continue in the same flowing style, and note that this last phrase (measures 44-47) repeats, ending in a quiet sigh. Hold the fermata long enough to let the harmony fade gently away.

ALL OF ME

Words and Music by JOHN STEPHENS
and TOBY GAD

Moderately, with feeling

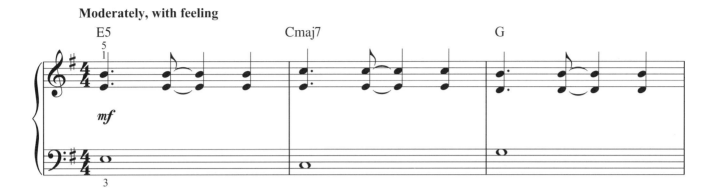

What would I do with-out your smart mouth draw- in' me

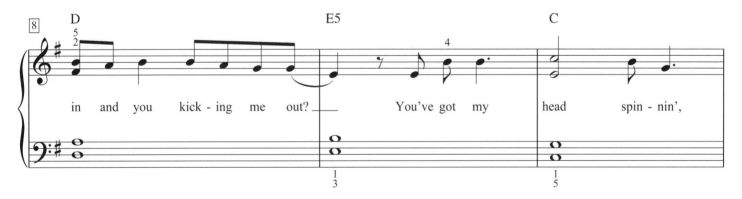

in and you kick- ing me out? You've got my head spin - nin',

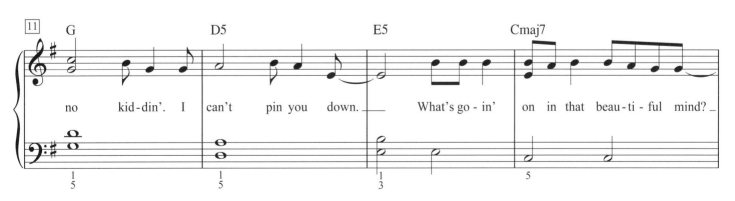

no kid-din'. I can't pin you down. What's go- in' on in that beau-ti- ful mind?

JAR OF HEARTS

Christina Perri's first hit, "Jar of Hearts" is a beautiful piano ballad. The right hand plays in the middle range of the keyboard, near middle C. The left hand plays single bass notes or 5ths. While simply constructed, the song still has a deeply dramatic feel. Measures 5-8 are almost the same as measures 1-4.

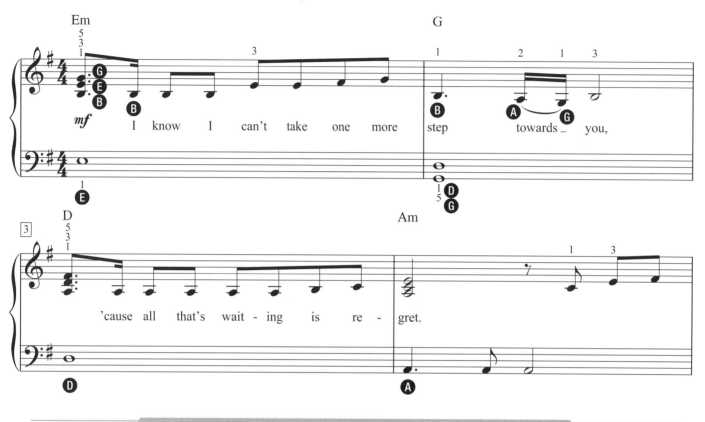

The left hand gets busier in measures 9-12. The fingering can help you move around the keyboard smoothly. Still playing 5ths and single notes, use the chord symbols above the treble staff as a guide to finding any notes you're unsure of.

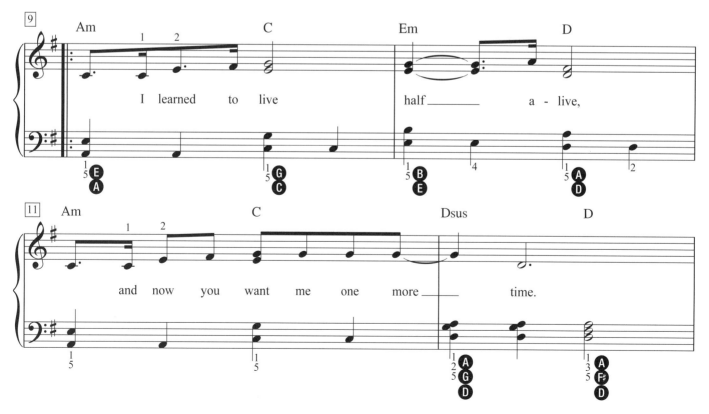

The chorus is also simply constructed, and stays in the mid-range of the keyboard. The left hand is a bit easier than the previous measures, in that the 3rds and 5ths are repeating quarter notes. This helps when playing hands together, with the left hand falling squarely on each beat. Measures 17-20 are a repeat of measures 13-16.

The eight-measure first ending is its own short section. You'll find the left hand familiar, but the right hand moves around a bit. Following the fingering will be a big help, so as you work on this section, play slowly at first, memorizing the fingering as you learn the notes.

At the second ending, the left hand has some colorful chromatic movement and some syncopation. Note that your left-hand thumb is anchored on the B just below middle C, and the lower notes move by half step, as marked in the example below.

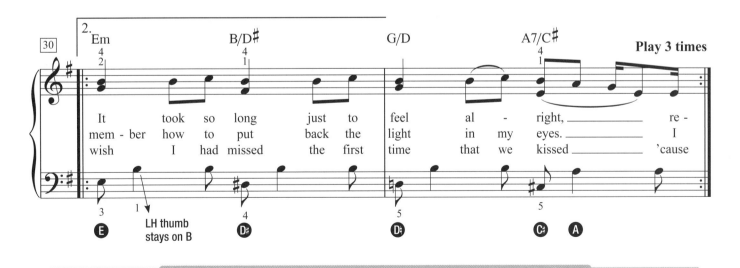

The D.S al Coda sends you back to the refrain, and then the coda. Note that your left hand shifts to middle C in measure 38 to reach the ledger line notes D♯ and F♯.

JAR OF HEARTS

Words and Music by BARRETT YERETSIAN,
CHRISTINA PERRI and DREW LAWRENCE

Moderate Ballad

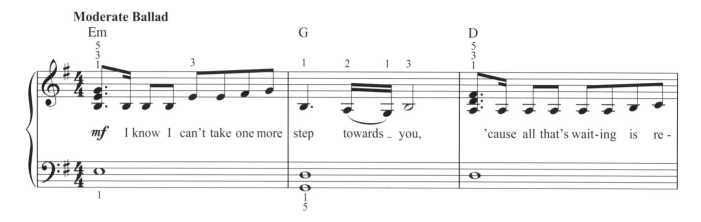

SOMEONE LIKE YOU

This old-school piano ballad was recorded by Adele with piano as the only accompaniment. The simple and plaintive sound of keyboard and vocal fits the lyrics perfectly. The four-measure introduction provides most of the material you'll need to play the song.

The chord structure is C-Em/B-Am-F. This progression is repeated three more times through the verse. In the introduction, the chords are presented as 5ths and 6ths. The right hand also plays these chords in an arpeggiated, or broken chord pattern. Note the similar notes between the chords. The right hand should be relaxed, but still playing each 16th note clearly. No rushing here—enjoy the beautiful chords unfolding on each beat of the music.

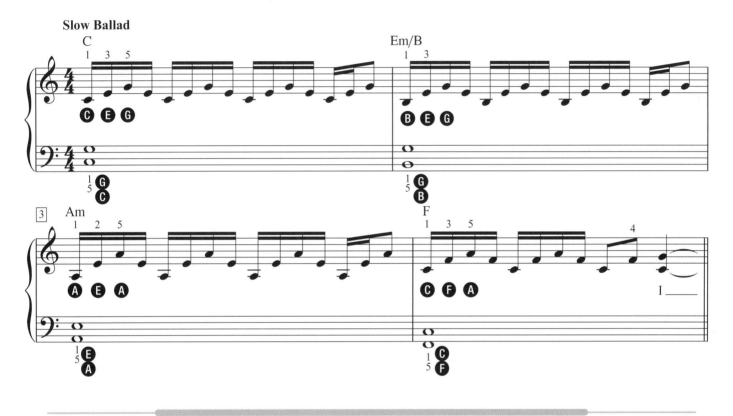

When the lyrics enter at measure 5, the right hand plays melody. The left hand plays the same 5ths and 6ths, but now, the notes are played individually, instead of together. The syncopated rhythm helps move this slow ballad forward. The song continues in this style, right-hand melody and left-hand syncopated pattern through measure 16. Look at the counting written in, and perhaps spend a little time with left hand alone, or left hand with the online audio, to become familiar with the rhythm and determine where the melody notes fit.

Measures 17-21 provide a short piano interlude. It looks very similar to the introduction, but uses the chord progression G-Am-F, played twice.

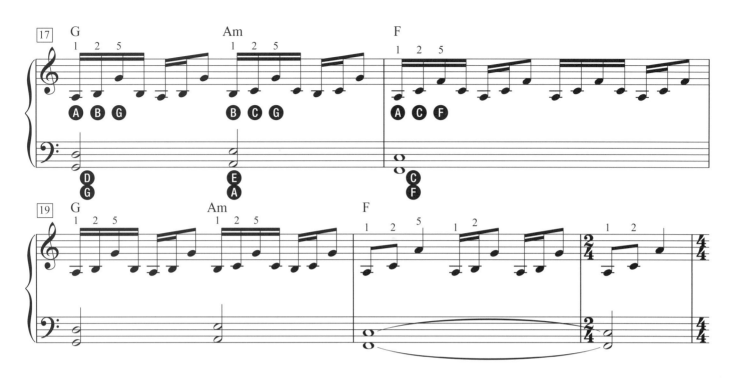

At the chorus, beginning in measure 22, the chord progression from the beginning of the song returns, with one small change. Instead of Em/B, you'll play G. The chords change faster in the chorus, twice per measure instead of only one chord per measure. The left hand is less syncopated in the chorus, and there's a nice descending line. Use your left-hand fifth finger to play the bass notes, stretching as needed. Those notes are easy to find if you use the chord symbols above the treble staff for help.

The arrangement ends with four measures of piano solo again, which will be familiar to you. Take your time and stretch the tempo at the *rit.*, letting the last notes linger under the fermata.

SOMEONE LIKE YOU

Words and Music by ADELE ADKINS
and DAN WILSON

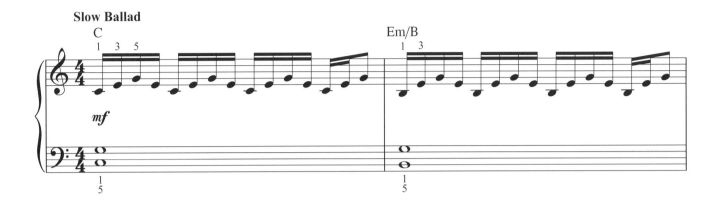

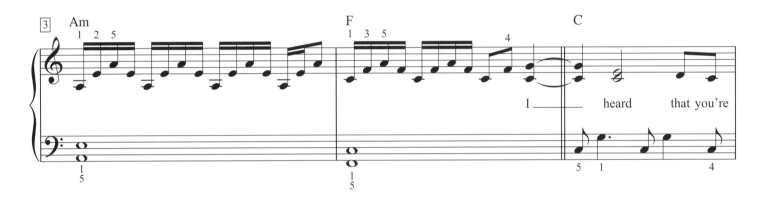

JUST GIVE ME A REASON

Pink's romantic pop ballad begins and ends with a piano solo. The simple melody line really shines, accompanied by a rather spare left-hand part, starting above middle C and playing unadorned intervals, leading right into the verse. Look ahead to the ending to see that these measures return.

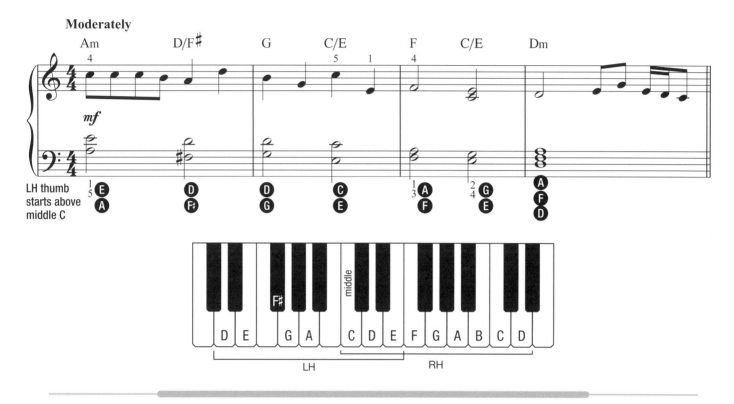

The 16-measure verse can be divided into two parts, measures 5-12, and measures 13-20. Let's take a look at the first part. Your left hand harmonizes with only three chords, C, F, and Am. Right hand stays with a simple melody line; single notes sometimes embellished with middle C.

The second half of the verse, beginning at measure 13, sees the addition of two more chords, D/F# and G, both appearing earlier in the introduction, so the left hand should look familiar. The right hand moves higher up the keyboard here, so switch your thumb to E, enabling you to make a smooth transition. Measures 17-20 are almost the same as measures 13-16.

Now you've arrived at the emotion-packed chorus, beginning at measure 21. The chorus, just like the verse, can be divided into two sections of similar material. The left hand plays single notes, and the key here is to move your left-hand thumb down to the C below middle C. Now you'll be able to play all the left-hand notes easily, moving down by step. There's another slight fingering shift in measure 23. We've marked it below. Note also the intervals we've marked for the right hand. You'll shift slightly to play each measure, but use the fingering given for help with this.

Use the online audio as you study and learn the various sections, and challenge yourself as you put the song together one part at a time. Remember to slow down the tempo when needed to navigate new fingering or movement between sections, increasing to performance tempo as you feel comfortable.

JUST GIVE ME A REASON

Words and Music by ALECIA MOORE,
JEFF BHASKER and NATE RUESS

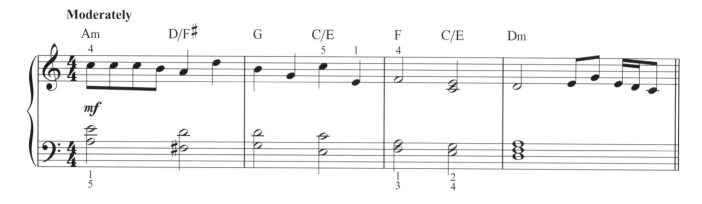

LET HER GO

The lyrics by British recording artist Passenger are melancholy, but its message is universal. In a folk rock style that translates well to the keyboard, you'll want to learn the chorus first. It's presented as an opening solo, and repeated later with lyrics.

The music box character of the introduction places the right hand high on the piano. If you're unfamiliar with the gentle syncopation here, listen to the audio for help. The left hand plays mostly single notes, and reflect the chord symbols above the treble staff. The harmony is simple: C-Cmaj7-Em-D.

When the chorus starts at measure 9, the right-hand syncopation gives way to a more straightforward rhythm. Also note that the right hand moves to a lower octave, making it easy to sing along. In measures 13-16, a change of finger on a repeated note makes it easy to shift lower on the keyboard. And notice too, left hand moves around quite a bit, with finger 5 moving to the root of each chord. The G chord is added to the harmonic structure.

At measure 18 there's a nifty two-measure riff that leads into the verse. It's just a D major chord, but the syncopation pulls you forward. Keep your arm and wrist relaxed at the repeated thirds in measure 20, and take a look at the left-hand fingering. The bass notes move down by step as the chords change. Following the pattern of the chorus, the 16-measure verse is really two 8-measure phrases that are almost exactly the same.

The D.S. al Coda takes you back to the chorus, and a short coda, to end our arrangement.

LET HER GO

Words and Music by
MICHAEL DAVID ROSENBERG

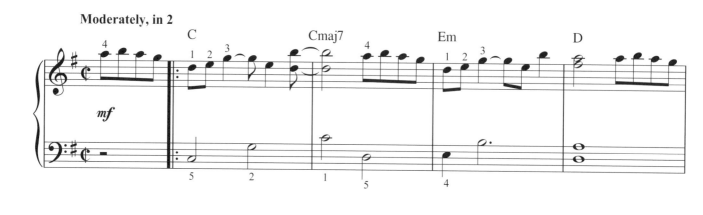

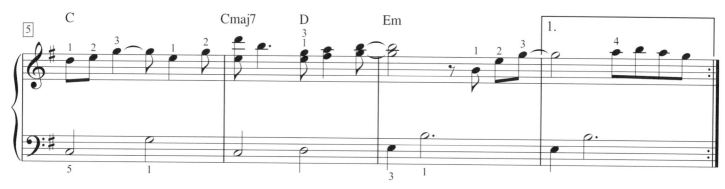

Well, you on-ly need the light when it's burn-in' low, ___ on-ly miss the sun when it starts to snow, _
high when you're feel-in' low, ___ on-ly hate the road when you're miss-in' home, _

on - ly know you love her when you let her go. ___

STAY

Rihanna's R&B ballad features piano right from the opening chords. Just four chords create a framework for the haunting melody and lyrics. Study the introduction below. The chord progression C-Dm-Am-Am7 uses all white keys. The left hand plays the root of the chords, while the right hand plays blocked chords in the middle of the keyboard. Notice how many of the notes repeat from chord to chord. For instance, middle C is played in every chord but one. There is only one note different between Am and Am7. A 7th chord adds the seventh note of the scale, in this case G. So adding a G to an Am chord creates Am7.

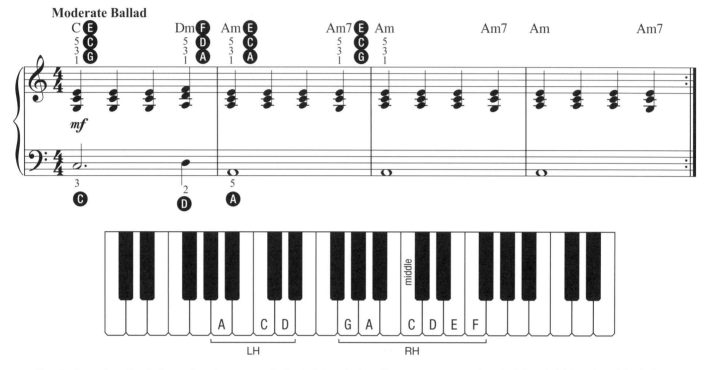

Continuing when the lyrics enter at measure 5, the left hand plays the same progression, but the right-hand part includes some added 3rds and 5ths to fill out the harmony. The right hand incorporates the opening chords into the lyric phrases. What makes this easy is the fact that the right hand stays in the middle of the keyboard. Following the fingering given will help with the slight shifts needed.

Leading into the chorus, starting at measure 21, there's a new chord, F6. This is an F chord with the sixth note of the scale added, in this case, a D. The D features prominently, as the melody note.

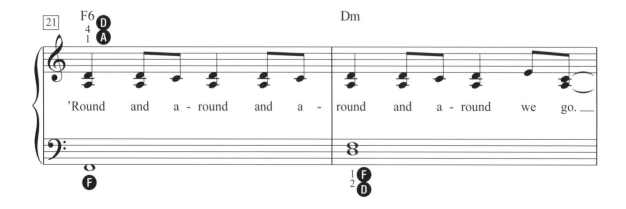

At the chorus (measure 29), the right hand moves between C and Dm chords, and a shift of finger on the D in the melody will help you to play this smoothly. This position change happens again in measures 33-36.

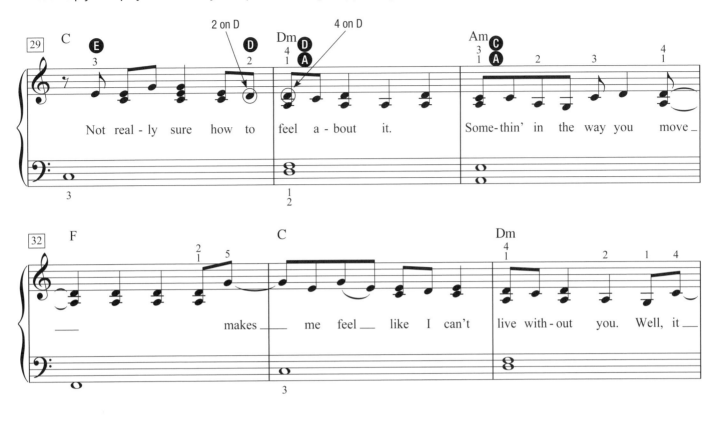

This beautiful ballad ends with solo piano chords much like the introduction, with one last poignant lyric phrase, ending on middle C.

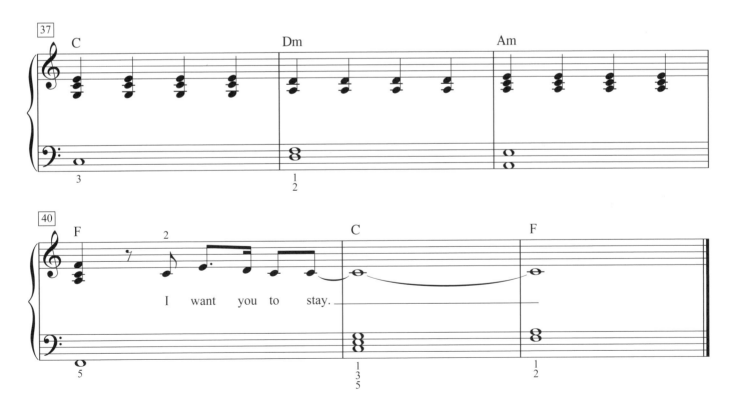

STAY

Words and Music by MIKKY EKKO
and JUSTIN PARKER

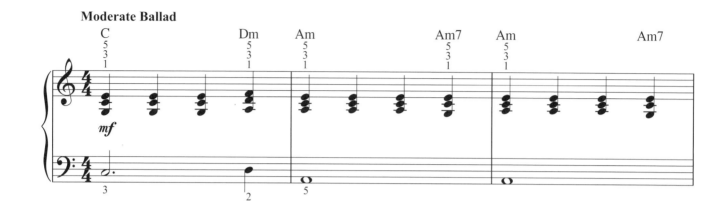

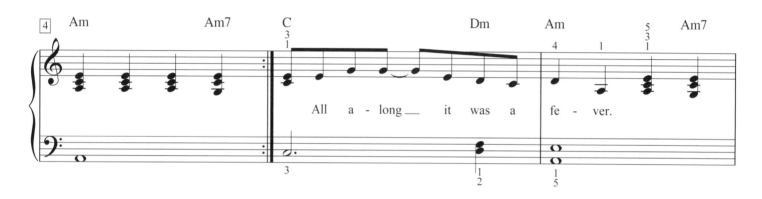

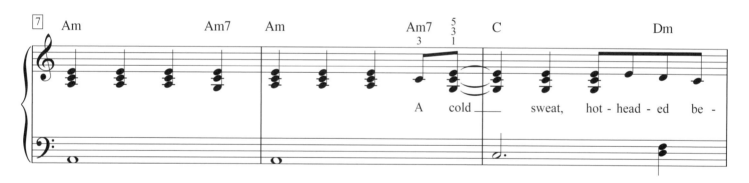

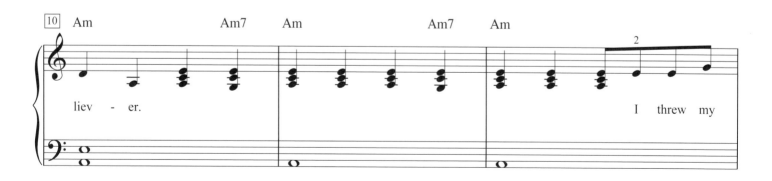

Not real - ly sure how to feel a - bout it.

Some - thin' in the way you move makes me feel like I can't

live with - out you. Well, it takes me all the way, I want you to stay.

I want you to stay.

WE ARE NEVER EVER GETTING BACK TOGETHER

Taylor Swift's catchy, Grammy-nominated break-up song is loads of fun. Let's jump right into the introduction. Your right hand stays at middle C, but the left hand moves from lower C, down to low G and then back up to C again. Use the upper G your left hand thumb plays as a type of home base as you move between the C and G. Use the online audio for help with rhythm and to get an idea of the quick tempo of this song.

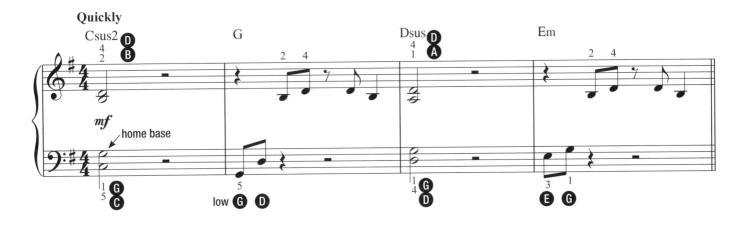

From the beginning of the song through the bridge, one four-measure chord progression is used, C-G-D-Em. Your left hand will have no trouble shifting between these chords, as they are close together on the keyboard. The right-hand melody is distinctive in its use of repeated notes. There's a story to tell, and the repeated notes allow it to unfold. Let your right hand bounce freely, allowing the repeated key to release fully. These four measures continue with very slight variation to form the remainder of the verse.

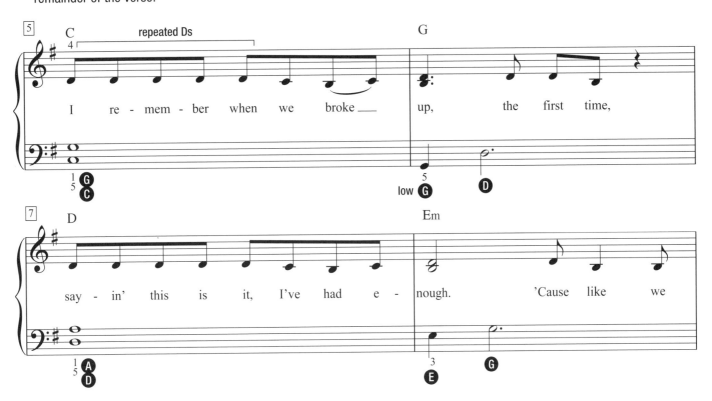

The bridge, starting at measure 21, and the lyric, "Ooh, ooh…" contains a two-measure hook that's infectious. Make sure you have a feel for the syncopation here, so check out the online audio to review if you're unsure of how this should go.

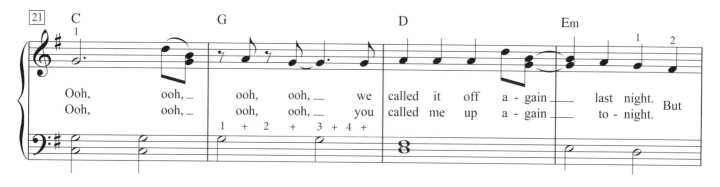

Once you hit the chorus at measure 29, the fun really starts. The syncopated melody fits the lyrics brilliantly, and once you've mastered measures 29-32 you'll breeze through the rest of the chorus. These four measures are repeated twice more, with slight variation.

You'll recognize the first ending, because it's just like the introduction. It sends you back for a second verse, and more of the story. Enjoy this second time through the bridge and chorus, and be sure to end with a definitive last two measures.

WE ARE NEVER EVER GETTING BACK TOGETHER

Words and Music by TAYLOR SWIFT,
SHELLBACK and MAX MARTIN

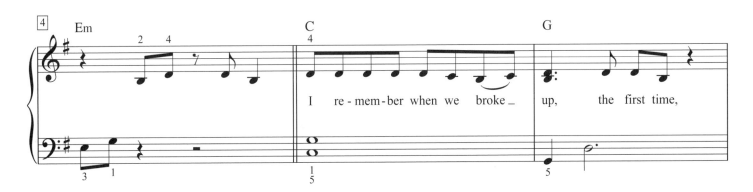

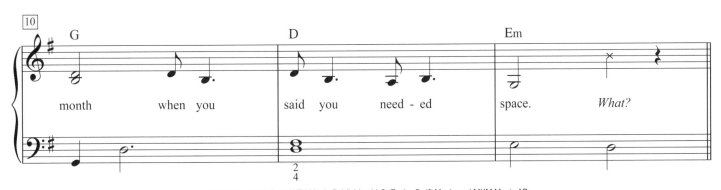

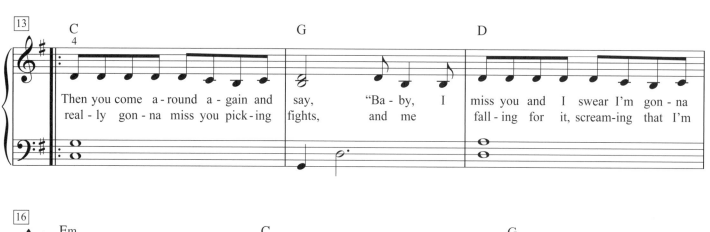

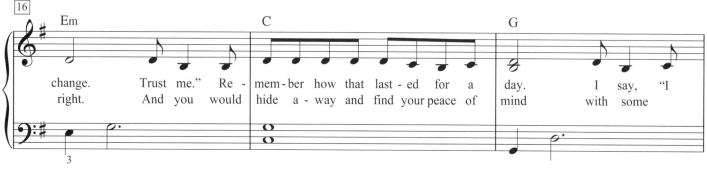

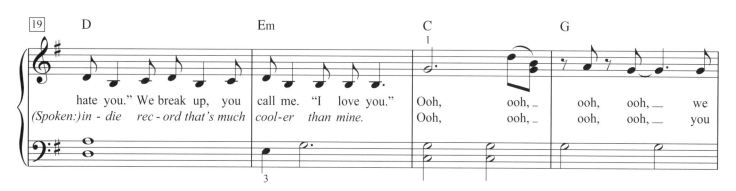

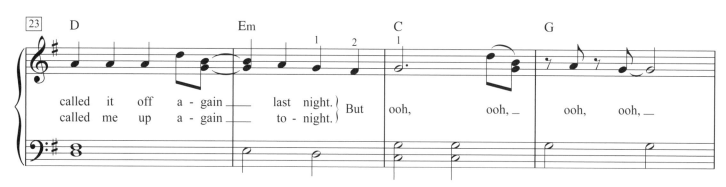

STAY WITH ME

Sam Smith's gospel-inspired ballad uses only three chords, Am-F-C, for both verse and chorus. Notice that in the introduction, both right and left hands are notated in the bass clef. This is because the right hand plays below middle C, and it's easier to read those notes in bass clef.

Listen carefully to be sure that when you play all four notes in the chord they sound at exactly the same time. Let your arm and fingers "sink" into the keys. This song moves at a slow to moderate pace, so take your time, and lean in a bit to the "and" of beat 4, to emphasize the syncopation there.

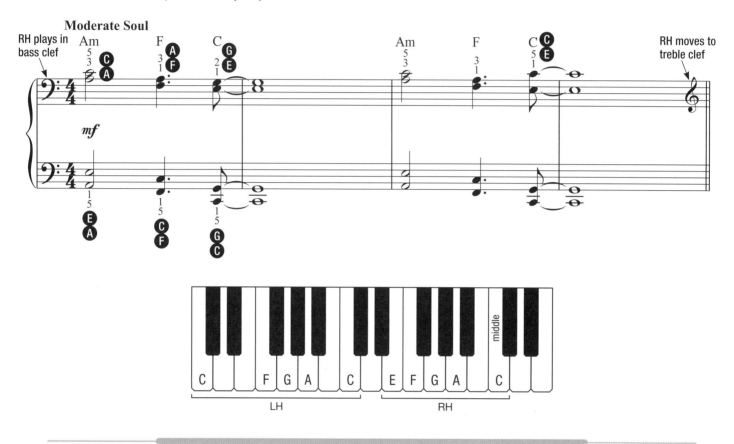

Continuing with the Am-F-C chord progression, when the lyrics enter at measure 5 your right hand moves back into treble clef. You're still in the middle of the keyboard, and thumb plays middle C.

Guess it's true, I'm not good at a one - night stand.

In measure 10, the right hand plays the melody note E in the bass clef, indicated by the slanted line.

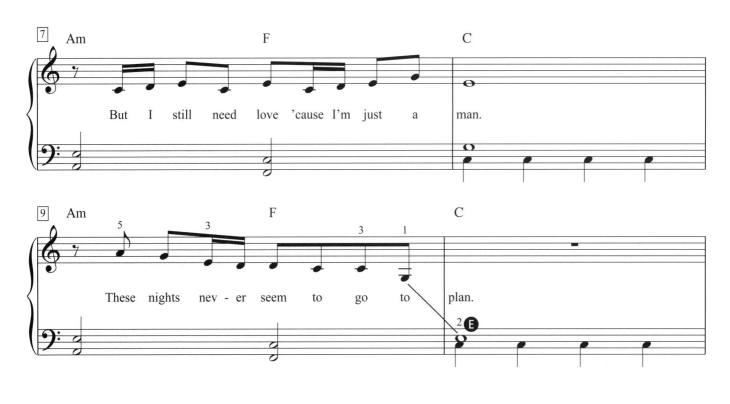

At the chorus, starting in measure 13, note the right-hand syncopation. We've written in the counting so it's easy to see where the hands play together, but if you're still unsure of the rhythm, play along with the online audio for a review.

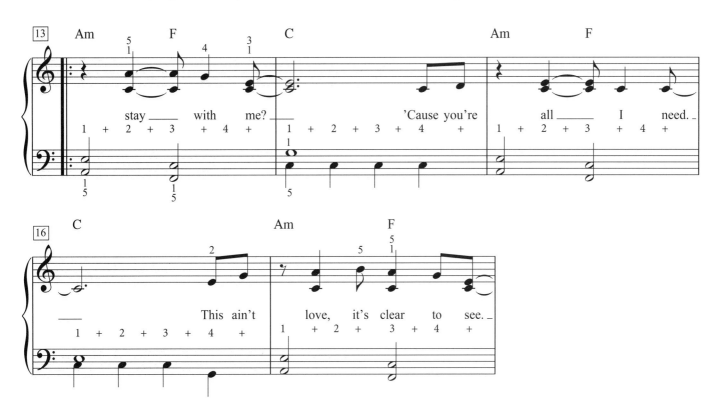

Repeat the chorus as indicated, and enjoy this soulful arrangement.

STAY WITH ME

Words and Music by SAM SMITH,
JAMES NAPIER, WILLIAM EDWARD PHILLIPS,
TOM PETTY and JEFF LYNNE

Moderate Soul

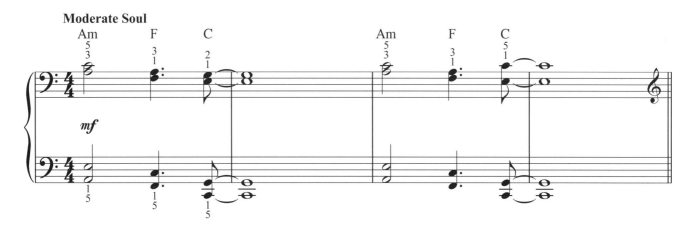

Guess it's true, I'm not good at a one-night stand.

But I still need love 'cause I'm just a man.

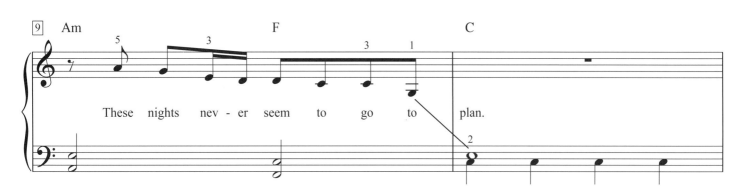

These nights nev-er seem to go to plan.

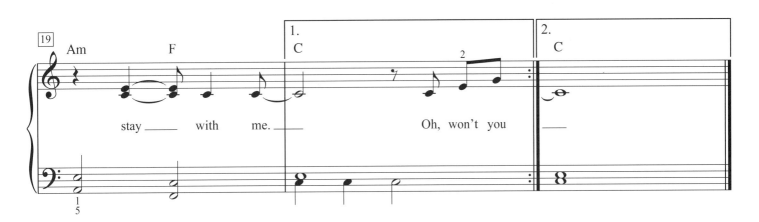

WHEN I WAS YOUR MAN

Singer-songwriter Bruno Mars uses the piano as the only accompaniment to his emotional ballad. The minimal style works well, and highlights the piano's mid-and lower range.

In the introduction there is just a bit a movement, D7-Dm7-C. In fact, in the very first measure, only one note changes. The F♯ moves to F-natural. Really sink into the keys to get this riff off the ground.

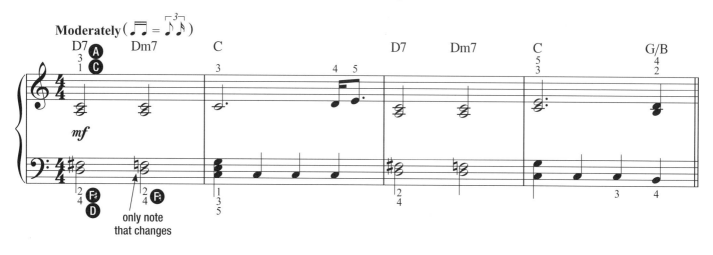

The verse beings at measure 5. The harmony expands to include Am, G and Em chords. The left hand stays in a relatively small area of the keyboard, and the bass notes reflect the chord symbols above the treble staff. The right hand plays a mostly single-note melody, filled out with some additional 3rds. Sing along as you learn the verse, and check out the online audio if you need a review.

The second half of the verse is almost the same as the first, so let's jump to the bridge at measure 13. You'll remember the plaintive, "Ooh, hoo." A little bit of syncopation edges that along, and the addition of B♭ in the harmony moves the song right into the chorus.

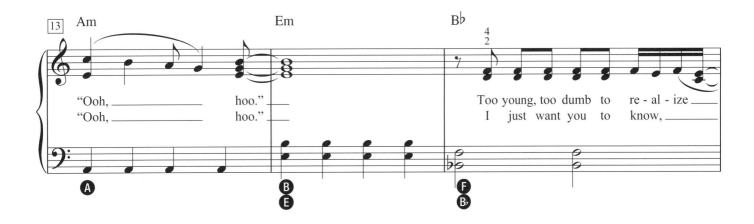

The chorus has a different, but simple, chord progression: C-F-G. Three similar phrases underscore the plaintive lyrics, with left hand playing 5ths, and right hand moving from lower to higher but staying pretty much within an octave range. Plenty of fingering is provided to enable you to play this section smoothly.

The repeat after the first ending sends you back to measure 5 for verse two. This time, take the second ending, which leads to an echo of the final phrase, bringing our arrangement to a close.

WHEN I WAS YOUR MAN

Words and Music by BRUNO MARS,
ARI LEVINE, PHILIP LAWRENCE
and ANDREW WYATT

Same bed, but it feels just a lit-tle bit big-ger now.
My pride, my e - go, my needs and my self - ish ways

Our song on the ra - di - o, but it don't sound the same.
caused a good strong wom - an like you to walk out my life.